Online Reputation Management

The 25 Things You Need To Know To Protect & Grow Your Business

By Robert David Gatchel

Founder & CEO of CyberMax Marketing

© 2017 Robert David Gatchel & CyberMax Marketing LLC   ALL RIGHTS RESERVED. No part of this book may be reproduced or transmitted in any form whatsoever, electronic, or mechanical, including photocopying, recording, or by any informational storage or retrieval system without the expressed written, dated and signed permission from the author.

LIMITS OF LIABILITY / DISCLAIMER OF WARRANTY:

The author and publisher of this book have used their best efforts in preparing this material. The author and publisher make no representation or warranties with respect to the accuracy, applicability, fitness, or completeness of the contents of this program. They disclaim any warranties (expressed or implied), merchantability, or fitness for any purpose. The author and publisher shall in no event be held liable for any loss or other damages, including but not limited to special, incidental, consequential, or other damages. As always, the advice of a competent legal, tax, accounting or other professional should be sought.

Table Of Contents

Table Of Contents 4

About The Author 6

What Is Online Reputation Management? 7

Why Is Online Reputation So Important? 9

How Do I Know What's Being Said About My Company Online? 11

Responding To Negative Reviews: Yes? No? 13

Can Slander On Social Media Be Removed? 16

Should I Hire A Lawyer? 17

Is There Anything I Can Do To Build A Positive Online Reputation? .. 18

How Do I Create Positive Online Reputation? I'm Busy! 20

Can Reputation Management Eliminate All Negative Reviews? 21

What Type Of Results Could My Business See? 22

Can A Consultant Guarantee Me A #1 Spot In Google? 23

What Does It Cost To Invest In Online Reputation Management? 24

How Long Does Online Reputation Management Take To Work? 25

Why Does It Take So Long? 25

How Do Search Engines Influence A Company's Online Reputation? . 27

Which Search Engines Online Reputation? 28

What Are Google Site Links? 29

What Are Google Knowledge Panels? 29

What Are Google Direct Answers? 30

What Is Search Engine Optimization? 31

Can I Be Notified When My Company Is Mentioned Online? 32

What Tools Can I Use To Help Me Track My Online Reputation? 33

What Social Networking Sites Are The Most Important? 34

Does My Website Represent My Business in The Best Possible Way? ...36

Does My Company's Reputation Stack Up To My Competitors? 37

The Next Steps 38

About The Author

Robert David Gatchel is an Internet marketing pioneer, entrepreneur, consultant, and is the founder of CyberMax Marketing LLC, a highly respected Internet marketing consulting agency. For the past 20 years, he's built several highly successful businesses online, generating millions of dollars in sales in the process. He's best known as a trusted online marketing advisor helping online startups and multi-million dollar corporations leverage the marketing power of the Internet to build thriving businesses.

As a consultant to several bestselling authors, he helped successfully market their books online, with many of these books hitting the top spots in the Amazon.com bestseller lists thanks to his specialized marketing strategies.

Robert has also co-authored two books on the subject of Internet marketing: "Multiple Streams of Internet Income" with legendary, bestselling author Robert G. Allen. And "Million Dollar Emails" with his colleague and noted online marketing authority Yanik Silver.

Robert's mission is to help ordinary people achieve extraordinary results by capitalizing on the power of the Internet to build their presence, their brand, and their business.

He can be reached at bob@cybermaxmarketing.com

What Is Online Reputation Management?

Online reputation management is nothing more than just having a system in place to monitor, protect and manage the online perception of your brand or company. For small business owners, it's the same as managing their reputation and customer expectations during the normal course of running their "face to face" business. For instance, when a local business owner has an unhappy customer, they typically try to turn around this bad experience "on the spot" at the time of the incident, or the reach out to the customer by phone, email, or engage them the next time the customer is in the store. This is true reputation management trying to keep the customer happy in hopes of maintaining future business.

Managing a business' reputation online isn't much different, but it can be very much important, because bad news & bad reviews can spread very quickly, damaging your business just as quickly. In today's mobile connected world, it's extremely easy for people to complain about a company online. There are numerous sites where reviews, comments, and opinions can be posted, and those comments can go very viral, very quickly. Online reputation management involves monitoring what is said about your company online, finding out what consumers are saying, creating content that guides the conversation in a positive way, and addressing – when necessary – unpleasant or negative experiences.

Business owners can do this on their own simply by searching for their brand online, identifying problems, and creating solutions in the form of press releases and other content. The challenge? Most business owners are so busy running their businesses to take the time necessary to conduct this process. They are often too busy to be searching for their brand online, let alone do the work to answer questions, handle complaints and stop the spread of reputation-damaging commentary online.

For this, online reputation management consultants are available that can take over the menial and time-consuming tasks. Using unique specialized online marketing methods & tools, online reputation management consultants can identify problems sooner and know how to fix them when they occur. And because of that, more and more businesses are starting to use them.

Why Is Online Reputation So Important?

Business owners often ask this before they even know what online reputation management really is! In fact, most businesses don't realize - until it's too late to stop the damage - how important it is to have a system in place to protect their brand and keep the perception of their business online in good standing.

Even after business owners understand this concept, they sometimes mistakenly think that because all of this activity is online, that it has no effect (or is not as important) as their reputation out "in the real world." They couldn't be more wrong.

What people are saying online today is everything, and it should *mean* everything to the business owner. Some might think that because they don't have an online business, that their online reputation isn't important. That's wrong & could be dangerous to the business. Even when customers are going to visit a physical location to purchase a product or use a service, they look online before they go. They see what people are saying, they take these reviews and comments into great consideration before deciding where or what to buy, and it seriously influences their future purchases.

This is why online reputation management is so important. Because even when business owners don't know it, people are out there talking about them. Those conversations, tweets, reviews & complaints are making their way to the top of the search engines; so not only can other consumers see them, they might be the only things customers and prospects see about a particular brand or business. If those conversations and reviews are negative, they can ruin a company. But if they are positive, they can significantly increase revenue for ANY business.

How Do I Know What's Being Said About My Company Online?

Of course, once business owners finally realize that people are out there talking about them and their business, they want to find out what it is people are saying. The easiest way to do this is to start by searching for information on the company in the major search engines. Google, Yahoo, and Bing are the biggest search engines, and the best ones to start any search.

Business owners can start by simply searching for the company name and the names of products or services they offer on the search engines. The best way is to take those terms and ad the term "review" as part of the search. This will provide search results on review sites such as Yelp, TripAdvisor, HomeAdvisor, Angie's List, etc. These reviews are often detailed and written by the customer, so business owners can see exactly what people are saying, and the experiences they had.

Note: when searching for your own brand or business with a search engine, it's important that you become "anonymous". Google and the other major search engines have become so technologically advanced, that they track your history and provide search results based on what you might be the most interested in. While this is convenient for the average search, it's not very helpful when you're searching for reputation management purposes.

This is because you want to know exactly what search results will appear when the average person searches for your business. In order to do this, you need to log out of any search engine accounts and turn off the personalized search option in the search engines. Better yet, you can do to an "incognito" or "private" browsing session on your web browser to do the same thing.

When trying to find out what people are saying about your business, it's also important to look at the number one ranking in all the search engines. Is it your website? Is it a press release? Is it something you or your company created and published? If not, you may have your first problem with your online reputation.

Responding To Negative Reviews: Yes? No?

Whenever a business owner sees that there's a bad review about them online, the first thing they want to do is get online and respond to the review. This can be good or bad, and it depends on how this is handled Sometimes business owners can become so inflamed by a bad review, especially when it's untrue, that they want to attack the attacker and get into a "battle of words" online.

This is *not* the way to respond to any negative reviews. And in fact, in some cases, it is best not to respond to them at all, for reasons I will explain in a moment. So how do you know when to respond, and when not to?

One of the key concepts in understanding this is to determine if the business was in the wrong and if there's a solution to the problem. For example, a customer tries to use two coupons at a grocery store and is told by the cashier that they can only use one at a time. The customer goes online and writes a negative review, stating that they'd never been told about the policy before and has in fact used multiple coupons at once before at that location. Once the review is online, it's there for anyone to see. And if there's a solution, it may be appropriate to respond to the review.

The grocery store owner could reply to the review, apologizing for the mistake, explaining that they were in training and confused the store policy. Or, the grocery store owner could reply to the review, explaining that using multiple coupons was once allowed at the store, but the policy had been changed recently. But doing this in a positive and proactive way is the key here. This is not to place to tell the customer they were wrong, or question their motives, or personally attack them.

When replying to reviews, it's very important that an apology is always followed up with a proactive solution, when possible. In this case, it would most likely be a simple matter of refunding the customer for the coupon amount or even sending them many coupons in the mail. A free item could also be offered to the customer the next time they're in the store. Any of these solutions would make the customer feel appreciated and listened to and would help both the business and the business' online reputation. The most important thing is that the customer wants to be heard, and responding appropriately and proactively can do this.

When the business owner is not in the wrong, and there is no real solution, there is no need to reply to the review or complaint. This happens most often when a customer simply did not get what they want, regardless of the policy, and/or they simply wanted to defame the business online. It can even happen when competitors give unfair negative reviews. It's unfortunate, but it does happen.

When it does, it is best just to let it lie and do nothing. Not only will engaging with these customers start a war that there's really no way for the business owner to win, but the very start of that battle will make the business owner look bad in the eyes of other customers. Even worse, continuing an online debate only continues to push that review to the top of the search engine ranks. When the business owner lets the review go, the search engines will too and soon, it will get lost in the shuffle.

Can Slander On Social Media Be Removed?

Social networking sites are a business owner's best friend, but they can also be their worst enemy. Social networking allows business owners to interact with their customers directly, often in a forum that the business owners control. But when a customer has posted a slanderous tweet, status update, or another form of comment or review that the business owner can't control, it can be difficult to get it taken down.

Unless the comment has violated the terms of service of the site, often the website will err on the side of the consumer. This is because these sites were designed with the intent of sharing information, and that includes among consumers. However, when the comments are outright abusive or can be shown to be slanderous and untrue, sometimes the commenter will be found in violation of the site's terms agreement, and the comment will be taken down.

Instead of focusing their efforts on having negative reviews or slander taken down, it is best for business owners to combat the problem with actively working to generate and encourage more positive reviews and positive online feedback that will overtake the negative.

Should I Hire A Lawyer?

If someone was to slander a business "in the real world," the first instinct the business owner might have is to hire a lawyer. And in the most persistent of cases, this might be a good idea. But it's never a good idea when the slander or negative comments are being made online.

Hiring a lawyer is an expensive process, not to mention a long one. By the time any real settlement or judgment is made, the slander would have gone away on its own online. And by continuing to bring attention and press to it, it will only keep the slander in the top search engine results longer. That means more people will be talking about it more often – the exact opposite of the desired result in this situation.

Is There Anything I Can Do To Build A Positive Online Reputation?

Yes! And in fact, the best way to combat negativity online is to create positivity. Business owners can do this in a number of ways.

Create a website with top-notch content that includes not only promotional pages and material but also helpful hints and tips and news about the industry. A good website, complete with keywords and SEO tactics is a business owner's number one defense against a negative online reputation.

Create a blog. This is more content and more information that the search engines can pick up and place high in their search rankings. Even more importantly, it is information that the business owner controls, so it's all creating positivity. Blogs can be used to provide up to date information and current news.

Register the business with as many local online directories as possible and keep listings current! Claiming the business name across all online directories has two purposes. The first is that it's yet another online location that the business owner can claim and that will help them get higher in the search engine rankings. It's also information that the business owner controls, which against helps create an online reputation. This is helpful because when customers can't find anything about a business online, they're apt not to trust it. Registering with online directories is also beneficial because if it is left open, someone else can claim it and use it to defame the business.

Create a profile across all social networking platforms. This will again, claim a space for the business high in the search engine results, and it also gives business owners a chance to directly interact with their customers.

Monitor social networks for mentions. Social media doesn't do business owners any good if they're not paying attention to what people are saying. It's important not only to blast the social network audience with solid and valuable information but also interact with followers. Business owners need to pay special attention when they're directly mentioned by anyone on social media and reply when they are.

Publish press releases. Press releases can be published and shared online very quickly. Creating a press release is an opportunity for business owners to tell their customers about major sales, new arrivals, and major news in the industry. And, just like all online content, press releases give the business owner one more place in the search rankings; and it's a place they control what's being said.

How Do I Create Positive Online Reputation? I'm Busy!

This is one of the biggest questions business owners have when they realize just how much time it can actually take to create, build, and protect an online reputation. And it's a valid one.

It's true that creating a positive online reputation does take time, and not only initially. Once a positive reputation has been established, it takes a constant effort to monitor, protect and maintain that reputation. And it's understandable that business owners just don't have the kind of time it takes to put in that work when they're busy running a great business. It's for this reason that more and more businesses are relying on online reputation management consultants to do the heavy lifting for them. Hiring an online reputation management consultant should not be considered an expense, it should be considered a direct investment to the business!

These professionals scour the web, creating profiles and gaining followers. They know how to find out what people are saying, and they know how to fix it when they find something negative. They know what positive content needs to be created to help the business place higher in the search engine rankings, and they can create it all.

The fees of a professional online reputation management consultant are minimal, but in today's online world, they're invaluable.

Can Reputation Management Eliminate All Negative Reviews?

While consultants can be helpful, it's important that business owners remain realistic. While consultants are experts, they don't have total control over the actions of others. When consultants find negative reviews, they will send a request to the webmaster, asking them to remove the review with a brief explanation of why they're making the request. After the request is made, it is up to the discretion of the webmaster whether or not the review is removed. It is their website after all, and for the most part, they're allowed to put whatever they want on it.

What Type Of Results Could My Business See?

Of course, no business owner wants to invest in something that's not going to give them results, but there's really no way to ever guarantee 100% accuracy with reputation management campaigns. The results will vary depending on the current state of the business' online reputation, how urgent the situation is, and how much new content needs to be created.

However, there are some things any business owner can expect out of a consultant. They should bring with them expert advice within the areas of brand and reputation management, they should report anything they find in a timely manner and sit down with the owner to decide how to deal with issues, and the business owner should be kept up to date at all times about the status of the project.

Can A Consultant Guarantee Me A #1 Spot In Google?

Page rankings and a business' online reputation go hand in hand, and to keep a positive reputation online, holding the #1 spot in Google's search results is a goal for any business owner. But, no business owner can guarantee a spot in #1, and neither can any consultant. In fact, Google themselves state that the number one spot cannot be guaranteed to anyone at any time, due to the fact that the algorithms are always changing and that spot is always in a state of flux.

But while business owners shouldn't hire a consultant expecting that they'll soon claim the top spot in Google, they should be wary of any consultant who guarantees such results – especially if they claim to have a priority or special relationship with Google. It simply isn't true.

What Does It Cost To Invest In Online Reputation Management?

Again, there is no one answer to this, and every case will be different. Spending the time to find out what consumers are saying about a particular brand or product online doesn't cost any more at all, and theoretically, a business owner could take care of most reputation management tasks on their own and with very little cost.

But in actuality, there is a cost attached. Even if the owner did it themselves, the cost there is still time – time that business owners don't typically have. Hiring a consultant can cost a business anywhere from $500 to $30,000 per month, depending on how big their company is, and how much damage has already been done. There may also be small fees associated with things like online directories, which will help a business' online reputation in the end.

In most cases, online reputation management is a very affordable undertaking for most business owners, even when they hire the help of a consultant.

How Long Does Online Reputation Management Take To Work?

All businesses are unique, and so too are their online reputations. Because of this, there's really no way to tell how long a reputation management campaign will take for any one business, without knowing the full extent of their current online reputation. If a company has little to no online reputation when they hire a consultant, it can take as little as just a few weeks to build up that reputation. However, if there is a lot of slander or negative content out there about the business, it could take as long as a year.

Why Does It Take So Long?

While managing an online reputation is important, it's definitely not something that happens overnight. One of the reasons why a campaign may take longer than a business owner was expecting is simply because there's a lot of work to be done on different websites. A consultant must visit all the different social media sites and set up profiles and pages for the business. Then they must also visit all the local online directories and claim the business on each of these, as well as set up a profile. The consultant may even have to set up a blog, or a website for the business.

All of these efforts are so that the content out there about the company is good, and more importantly, that it outweighs any negative content that may be out there. Putting in this kind of work simply takes time.

Another reason why it can take so long before business owners start seeing results from their online reputation campaign is that search engines don't rank new sites very high in the results. So if a blog or website is made, it's going to take time before the search engines give it a high ranking that's above negative content.

How Do Search Engines Influence A Company's Online Reputation?

When a business owner thinks about their online reputation, it's natural to first think about the commenters or reviewers – those people who are actually out there, saying things about the company. But there's more to it than that. Because before a commenter's remark can be put online, the search engines need to decide where to place that remark within their own search rankings.

Search engines are like the gatekeepers of the internet. Using complex algorithms, they decide what content is most important and relevant to users, and will place content accordingly so in the results pages. When business owners start thinking like this, they realize just how large of a role search engines hold in online reputation campaigns, and just how important they are.

Which Search Engines Online Reputation?

Long gone are the days of just having an option of one or two search engines. Today, people can find a search engine just about anywhere they look, and some are even specialized to specific industries or topics. But while all search engines will affect an online reputation to a degree, there are some that are bigger than others and as such, have more of an impact.

Think about it. If millions of people are using Google every day, that's potentially millions of people that could come across any one particular business. But if only thousands of people are using a smaller search engine, such as Dogpile, fewer people will have access to that one business. The same works for comments and reviews. When trying to fix or build an online reputation, it's important to start with the larger search engines and work down to the smaller ones.

So where does one start? Google is the main search engine, with the highest number of users. They have over 1 trillion pages in their index and they grow by the billions every day. Yahoo, Bing, etc. are the next biggest search engines after Google.

What Are Google Site Links?

When a search is performed for a big website or a big business, Google will often provide the link to the home page first, and then underneath provide a number of links to other pages within that website. These are known as site links and they're helpful to business owners for a number of reasons. This automated process analyzes the link structure of the website and to save visitors time, will provide them with the main links so it's easier for them to navigate through a website. They give the website owner greater control of the search results page and are thought to be extremely beneficial for building a company or website's reputation.

What Are Google Knowledge Panels?

Just like a website with Google site links will be more recognizable and easily identifiable as the top search result, so too are Google knowledge panels. These panels appear at the side of the page after a user has searched for a particular business or keyword. The panels display basic information, such as the company's name and industry along with contact information, which can help customers discover and learn more about any business. Because these panels make it easier for users to find your website and business, and because they appear so prominently on the page, they are important to a company's online reputation.

What Are Google Direct Answers?

Google is trying to save users time in their search so, instead of forcing them to look through multiple websites before finding their search query, at times Google will provide a Direct Answers box. This box appears before all the other search results and gives a brief explanation or description of the searched term. This helps searchers immensely, but it can help business owners, too.

Business owners want to be seen as the expert in their industry, the authoritative voice on the matter. When a portion of their web page is displayed in a Google Direct Answers box, it only helps reinforce the idea that they are the leading voice on the matter. Also, in addition to the answer, Google also places a link back to the page where the answer was taken from, increasing how prominently sites appear in the search results, and the visibility those sites are given.

What Is Search Engine Optimization?

Of course, the search engines don't have actual people scouring the web every day, ranking pages and websites. This would be an impossible task. Instead, they have little robot "spiders" that go out, look for key components of websites, and rank those sites accordingly in the search engine results. Because these spiders are electronic, users need to enter information that they'll understand and be able to identify. This is known as search engine optimization.

When you break down the phrase, search engine optimization is just optimizing – making the best use out of – a website so that it can be recognized by the search engines. There are a number of SEO tactics that reputation consultants, web hosts, and content developers use in order to make their sites seen by the search engines.

One of the biggest tactics is to use keywords throughout the site. These are the words users will enter into a search engine when they're looking for a specific topic, and they're one of the best SEO tactics that can be used. Links, either internally or to external sites, are another way that sites can be optimized so that they can be easily identified by the search engines. This is also a combination of art & science and should be handled by a professional, because BAD SEO can be worse than NO SEO!

Can I Be Notified When My Company Is Mentioned Online?

Of course, one of the tasks that require the most time when building and managing an online reputation is trying to stay on top of what everyone is saying about the company, brand, product, or service. And not only does this need to be done at the very beginning of an online reputation campaign, it needs to be done regularly throughout the campaign; and it needs to be regularly done once the campaign is thought to be over, for the most part. Otherwise, those comments and reviews are just going to pile up again.

Thankfully, there's an easy way to do this. Business owners simply need to subscribe to Google Alerts, Social Mention, Brandwatch, or any other monitoring tools they think will be useful. These tools scour the web every single day and send an email notification to the business owner when the keyword (company's name or brand) is used. This gives the business owner a daily look at what users are saying about them and their company and alerts them right away that there's a problem that may need to be fixed.

Some online reputation management consultants also have proprietary software solutions that can act as a "one-stop shop" - where all of these features can be found in one interface, that also allows business owners to control the information they post from one portal.

What Tools Can I Use To Help Me Track My Online Reputation?

There are so many tools available to business owners that have been created with the sole intent of helping those business owners stay on top of their reputation and what people are saying about them. Yahoo Alerts works very similarly to Google Alerts, and Feedreader is also a great way to get entire articles that have been posted about the company or brand. Social Mention is a great way to see what people are saying across all social networking sites, while Twitter search and Facebook search are functions within social platforms that will help business owners make better use of them.

Of course, there are also all of the local online directories and the many different social media sites that business owners should be a part of. There are tons of tools designed specifically to help business owners track their online reputation, and all business owners should be using at least a few of them.

What Social Networking Sites Are The Most Important?

This will largely depend on the company and the industry the company is in. And while some consultants may advise that every business be present on every social networking platform, this isn't necessary in all cases. For instance, YouTube videos get a very high ranking in the search engine results because it's such a huge website. But it may not be appropriate for all businesses to have a YouTube channel. In some cases, it will simply be a matter of the business owner's discretion and where they want to appear.

There are some social networking sites that *all* businesses should be on. Facebook is the largest social networking site there is, so it's important that all business owners at least claim a page for their business, if not a personal profile. In addition, LinkedIn is known for being a social networking platform for professionals and is to be used as a place for networking with other professionals in the industry and like-minded individuals. Because of this, every business should also have a LinkedIn company page.

And then there are the industry-specific social networking sites. These include platforms such as ActiveRain, a website designed to bring real estate agents, mortgage brokers, and others in the real estate market together. Avvo on the other hand is a social networking site designed to connect lawyers with those seeking legal help and advice. When there are social networking sites such as these that are designed for specific industries, business owners in that industry should make it a point to be a member and to be active, on those platforms.

Does My Website Represent My Business in The Best Possible Way?

This is a question that most business owners don't think to ask, but they should. And most don't think to ask because they believe that their website does, in fact, represent their business in the best possible way. After all, they put a great deal of thought into it when they created it, they may have even hired professionals to help them maintain that website, and it says everything they want it to say.

All of this could be true, and the company's website still does not represent the business in the best possible way. Maybe it's simply straightforward basic information with little engaging content. Or perhaps it's missing information that the business owner didn't even think to include. The biggest mistake though, is often that the company's website URL doesn't directly mirror the actual business name, making it difficult for people (and search engines) to find it.

A company's website is their first defense when it comes to online reputation, and so during any branding campaign, the website must be looked at with a very critical eye.

Does My Company's Reputation Stack Up To My Competitors?

Business owners must always be aware of their competition, what they're doing, and how the business stacks up to those of offering the same product or service. This holds true when it comes to the competition's online reputation as well.

Searching for a competitor's name or product can be very helpful and will show business owners instantly what people are saying about their competition. Business owners should look at the top search results, see if the results are positive or negative, and what exactly the piece of content is. This information will provide insight as to what the competition is doing right when it comes to their online reputation, and what they're getting wrong.

The Next Steps

Thank you for reading this book. I hope that you found it useful and that it has given you the information you need to help you better understand the importance of managing your online reputation and the strategies to employ to help you do just that.

If you would like additional assistance, please contact our agency at:

Robert David Gatchel
Founder of CyberMax Marketing LLC
http://CyberMaxMarketing.com
Email: info@CyberMaxMarketing.com

www.ingramcontent.com/pod-product-compliance
Lightning Source LLC
Chambersburg PA
CBHW071202240526
45470CB00017B/1231